From the
YOGA MAT
to the
Corner Office

A MINDFUL APPROACH TO BUSINESS SUCCESS

Yvonne James Furth and Molly Rudberg-Leshnock

HIGHPOINT
EXECUTIVE
PUBLISHING

NEW YORK • SAN FRANCISCO

From the Yoga Mat to the Corner Office:
A Mindful Approach to Business Success

This edition published by Highpoint Executive Publishing.

For information, write to info@highpointpubs.com.

First Edition

ISBN: 978-0-9891054-9-1

Library of Congress Cataloging-in-Publication Data

Furth, Yvonne James and Rudberg-Leshnock, Molly
From the Yoga Mat to the Corner Office: A Mindful Approach to Business Success

Summary: "This valuable illustrated guide integrates yoga concepts with the professional conversation and landscape. Using these principles, allowing readers to create a more successful professional and personal life." —Provided by publisher.

The authors hereby disclaim any liability for injury which may occur from any yoga practice or exercise contained herein.

ISBN: 978-0-9891054-9-1 (paperback)
1.Business 2. Personal Success

Library of Congress Control Number: 2014956724

Design by Sarah M. Clarehart

10 9 8 7 6 5 4 3 2 1

FROM THE YOGA MAT TO THE CORNER OFFICE

A MINDFUL APPROACH TO BUSINESS SUCCESS

CONTENTS

ACKNOWLEDGEMENTS

Our "attitude of gratitude" starts here. Thank you so much to everyone who helped to bring this idea to fruition. When we first met and started working together at Dominican University, we had no idea that this partnership would result in a project that would be this fulfilling for both of us. Thank you to the graduate students in the Dominican University Women's Leadership group, who responded so well to the lecture on "Balance in the Workplace" which eventually gave rise to this book. Thank you also to our yoga instructors and business mentors who helped to shape how we approach business and life challenges.

One of the most important elements of this book is the one-on-one research which we conducted with over 40 successful business professionals. Thank you to each of you who responded and participated in the research and who eventually allowed us to share your advice and your success stories. Special thank you to Tamara Johnson, Kim Bookless and Victoria Uecker for your invaluable input. This book would not be as rich in content without your help.

Thank you to Michael Roney, Sarah M. Clarehart, and the group from Highpoint Executive Publishing for all of your efforts in making *From the Yoga Mat to the Corner Office* happen. Your help and guidance throughout this process has been very professional and you have made the process pleasurable along the way.

Finally, thank you to our friends and our family. Especially our husbands, Glenn Furth and Brad Leshnock, for your love and support always. And, of course, our sons Andrew Furth, Alexander Furth, Joseph Leshnock, and William Leshnock who are our constant source of inspiration and awe. We are counting on you—the next generation—to continue to change the conversation in the workplace. And to continue living your lives in a mindful way.

— Yvonne James Furth and Molly Rudberg-Leshnock

DEDICATION

This book is dedicated to our parents Richard and Lynn Rudberg and Helma Hollis, for being the first to model these principles. And in loving memory of Laddie James.

INTRODUCTION

From the Yoga Mat to the Corner Office is a business book that integrates yoga principles with shared real-life experiences and expert opinions in order to change the conversation, culture, and definition of business success. Throughout this book, we cite research and quote numerous survey responses from successful business professionals in cutting-edge, global organizations, such as Google, Facebook, Walmart, Kohler, Wm. Wrigley, and others. Our mission is to integrate yoga concepts, such as building core strength, balance, and flexibility, into the professional conversation and landscape. Using these principles, we will help you clear the space needed to live a more centered professional and personal life.

A Mindful Approach

Yoga incorporates the concept of *mindfulness*—being aware of your own thoughts and feelings rather than judging them. Taken as a whole, a mindful approach to business provides a great path to success, not only in that environment but in your life. Increasingly, successful companies are using a mindful approach to increase employee welfare and productivity.

According to *Organizational Mindfulness: How Contemplative Practice Can Enhance Your Business* by Bird Pilatsky, bringing mindfulness to the workplace can yield many positive results, such as:

— lower stress levels;

— greater productivity;

— higher job satisfaction;

— improved employee health;

— an increased sense of purpose; and

— fewer feelings of isolation and alienation.

Whether you are a practicing yogi or someone who is just thinking about yoga's benefits, we are confident that you will find much valuable information here. If you are a seasoned yogi, you will appreciate the added perspective of what your daily practice can do to advance your professional goals. If you are new to yoga, this is a great way for you to get oriented and begin a lifelong practice that will pay dividends in achievement and happiness. As with any exercise program, please consult with your physician before beginning your yoga practice. To reduce the risk of injuries, yoga should always be practiced under the guidance of a professional instructor. Keep in mind that not all yoga poses are for everyone. Do what is right for you.

This book will serve you well regardless of your definition of business success. Your "corner office" could literally be the office of the CEO of a large corporation or peak success as a doctor, lawyer, CPA, teacher, and any other professional field. It also could mean building your own business success as an entrepreneur or a consultant. We offer tips and suggestions for how to clear the space needed to be successful in both your professional and personal life.

Survey and Results

As part of our discovery process around work and yoga, we conducted a survey of approximately forty women and men in mid- to high-level management/executive positions throughout the country. The intention of the survey was four-fold:

1. Discover what's going on in today's business world.

2. Unearth key issues our demographic is experiencing.

3. Prioritize our principles and confirm our theory.

4. Determine a benchmark for our book.

What we found was a business world that can be out of sync with the realities and needs of today's working professionals, with women and men alike seeking a greater mind/body/spirit conversation in the business environment. Ranging from three to more than thirty-five years in the working world, men and women ranked what they felt was needed to succeed in business in order of importance, with focus, stretching (getting out of your comfort zone), and strength leading the way. As you will see, these elements often interact with each other and sometimes overlap.

Our Personal Perspective

Yvonne James Furth, *Retired President/CEO, Draft Worldwide (Now FCB Global) and Executive Vice President of the Board of Directors, The Off The Street Club*

I joined Draft Worldwide in 1981 as an Assistant Account Executive and worked my way up the ranks to eventually become the President/CEO. During that time, my husband and

I raised two wonderful sons. Balancing that work life and home life was difficult. It was both wonderful and fast paced. Most working days felt nonstop. However, no matter how much or how far I ran, I always ended up in the same place.

After thirty years of experiencing constant intellectual and physical challenges in the world of advertising, I decided to retire. I've "been there, done that" in the corporate world. I've experienced firsthand what's missing. Now that I'm retired, I am committed to taking care of myself mentally, physically, and spiritually. And that's why I started practicing yoga. I began to learn the concepts of building core strength, balance, and flexibility, among many other yoga concepts, and I thought, "Why didn't I do this while I was working?" We are always looking for the silver bullet to tell us how to be successful at something. This seems to be one avenue toward a much more centered, balanced approach to business and to life.

Molly Rudberg-Leshnock, *Leadership Innovator, Organizational Alchemist, Life Coach–Molly Rudberg, LLC*

An entrepreneur at heart, I've been hustling for close to twenty years. Whether it was early on in my career with MRL Productions, partnering with organizations to develop outcome-driven, experiential meetings and events, or now as a catalyst of change for organizations and human beings. I have created this while sustaining my own health and happiness, a home, two young boys, a happy husband, teaching, writing, and supporting numerous nonprofits. All things I love! Yet, business and personal success has come with pain and struggles through the years. It was satisfying and successful one day and incredibly frustrating the next. Something in the roller-coaster ride of work and life had to give, and it wasn't going to be me!

As my business grew, so did my drive to balance the numerous dimensions of my life. I looked for ways to remain centered and peaceful. It wasn't until yoga was introduced to me that I found my solution. I found that, if I show up, do the hard work, remain flexible, and stay as centered as I can in the moment, I get stronger, wiser, and happier. This, to me, is the essence of success. I have heard others clamoring for the same thing: a deep desire to learn new ways to balance and blend the various important aspects of our lives in order to care for ourselves, families, and work. Such is the purpose of this book.

Begin the Journey

We are the professionals who overwork and overcommit, trying to keep up with a chaotic professional life that provides no outlet or opportunities for a balanced approach. Individually, and now in partnership, we utilize a more centered, peaceful approach to work and life via yoga principles and our mat. We stretch, flex, and sweat our way to success.

At the end of each chapter, we have included a section titled "Daily Practice." It contains suggestions for how you can incorporate these principles into your everyday life and help change the corporate conversation. We are offering up a different perspective and approach to work. By bringing you along on this journey, we wish to give you the tools you can use to create a more joyful, healthy business environment filled with centered, soul-filled success.

With a combined forty-five-plus years of successful corporate and entrepreneurial work under our belts, we've experienced firsthand what an uncentered approach to business can do to the spirit. We hope that, with this book, we'll inspire a new level of professional being and bring into the conversation the elements of yoga that have positively changed our business mind-set and, hopefully, yours.

Chapter 1

BREATHE

Use your breath to strengthen and steady your mind.

"Breathe. Let go. And remind yourself that this very moment is the only one you know you have for sure."

— Oprah Winfrey

Breath Control Pose: "Pranayama"

Breathing is just one critical element to remaining calm and centered in the face of business chaos and to being the strong center that gets you (and your company or your team) through tough situations. A practiced breathing technique reminds us we can approach challenging situations with peaceful, centered, well-intentioned solutions. A focus on breath is the basis for both successful yoga and business practices.

HOW TO DO IT

1. Sit in a comfortable position with legs crossed or in half-lotus position. Make sure your spine is straight. Closing your eyes, put your hands on your abdomen and chest to help feel the breath. Try to clear your mind. Listen to the air flowing in and out.

2. Breathe in. Try to actually visualize your breath as it makes its way through your nostrils, down your throat, into your lungs, and, from your lungs, throughout the rest of your body.

3. As you breathe out, visualize this process in reverse. Be sure to keep bringing your focus back, gently, if your attention wanders.

"I have succeeded in business during times without many of the softer qualities, but experience much more joy and teamwork when I incorporate humor, flexibility, balance and remember to breathe."

— **Gina Marotta,** *Happiness Advocate and Coach at Gina Marotta.com; Former Managing Director and Chicago Founder of StepUp Women's Network*

Breathe for Success

Breath is necessary. It revitalizes the mind, steadies the emotions, and allows for thoughtful reflection. Mindful, conscious breathing offers you an opportunity to slow down and focus on the current situation or challenge. You take in good and release bad. A breathing practice clears your mind and allows for illumination of your greatest self. This technique is critical to business success in that it allows you to peacefully and more artfully create, deliver, and delight in your work.

In Alexander Lowe's book, *The Voice of the Body,* he states the importance of breathing as the life support for our spirit as well as our soul. The reason that breathing is the main factor in the practice of yoga is that the "breath holds the secret to the highest bliss."

"Breath work is the first stop on the path to emotional resilience. Just a few simple deep breaths can center you before a meeting, a presentation, or a crucial conversation. This is more than just good practice—deep breathing brings oxygen to vital organs allowing them (ergo, you) to function more efficiently."

— **Emily Bennington**, *Author, Coach, Speaker, Leadership Consultant*

We live in an extremely fast-paced, technological world that is constantly spinning us in new directions. Yet, with this new pace, we are expected to continue delivering high-quality work and communication in a flawless, mindful way. This is expected no matter what the price to our sanity, ourselves, or our souls.

To realize the greatest benefit from breathing, you must first and foremost become *aware*. Most of us move through our day without much notice of the air we take in and release. With this lack of awareness, we are more likely to breathe in a shallow manner or simply not fully breathe in necessary—but stressful—moments. These limited and learned habits do not allow for healthy living. Therefore, mindful breathing is necessary to live and exercise our best selves. It's what allows for our feelings to flow smoothly and, if done well, move unobstructed through our bodies and minds. To become aware of our breath and how we breathe in this world will not only bring more peace to our own inner lives but to others around us as well.

Here are a few suggestions for how to incorporate mindful breathing into your personal and professional life in order to promote harmony and, ultimately, success:

1. Slow down. A common, universal experience we've all had is when technology gets the better of us. You might be working on a project, e-mail, or piece of very important communication and your computer freezes, shuts down, or just doesn't do what you expect it to do. Sound familiar? Instead of hitting numerous keys, turning the computer on and off (risking loss of your document), or even hitting your hard drive (Come on! We've all done it!), sit with this moment. Practice what this experience is providing: a gift that allows you to slow down. Notice the emotions it brings up and breathe through the frustration or stress. With this new approach comes a quieting of the mind and may even allow for some humor. With the gift of this new moment of breath and quiet, you can allow yourself to shift into a new energy and, ultimately, the way in which you approach the next moment.

2. Retreat, reflect, and relax. Connecting and mindfully building relationships with others enriches our lives in numerous, productive ways. When we feel close to colleagues, friends, lovers, parents, and siblings, we gain greater awareness of ourselves, promoting positive energy, harmony, and worth. We all have experienced a moment or two (or maybe four hundred!) when a relationship has tried us. It's in these moments that breath can be our ally and support system. The next time you feel frustrated or hurt or angry at someone close to you (even someone at work whom you feel failed you), practice becoming aware of your breath and, if needed, excuse yourself from any initial reaction or communication. Take a breath before taking action. As you relax, use breath as your friend. By allowing yourself the time to sit mindfully in the moment, you will approach the situation in a more peaceful, productive way.

3. Focus on the present moment. As we move through our professional lives, there is a possibility that we will encounter moments of trauma and despair. Whether this happens in our work environment, in our personal lives, or to others, when tragedy hits, we are impacted. Our minds play tricks on us and continue to play out tragedies, with the impact felt over and over. Bring your mind back to the present moment. Think about and feel your current situation and setting. See and feel the setting in which you are present. Take in only that moment … and breathe.

4. Soak in—and breathe out—your feelings. Allow all of your emotions to wash over you. Allow for fear, grief, stress, and sadness to reveal themselves. Breathe through these emotions, giving them life and energy. By allowing our emotions to reveal themselves, we refrain from building walls and plaque around our hearts.

5. Accept uncertainty. Tragedy and challenge, by nature, ask us to begin building walls of denial and doubt in the world. By extending breath into and out of our bodies, minds, and hearts, we continue to break down those walls and remain productive in our lives. The sooner we accept our current state of life, the sooner we can feel at peace.

Recent studies conducted at Massachusetts General Hospital document the positive impact deep breathing has on the body's ability to deal with stress and stressful situations. It can restore perspective, enable you to take a fresh look at a question or a problem, and come up with new solutions.

"One of the ways in which I have been able to continue with my work, even in the face of adversity and challenge, is by breathing through the discomfort. I am able to let go of what doesn't serve me and focus on what does."

— Emily Bennington, *Author, Coach, Speaker and Leadership Consultant*

6. Eliminate the stressful thoughts. In a recent article in *Forbes* magazine, Siimon Reynolds writes that the stresses in the workplace have never been higher.

He offers solutions in the form of a simple technique he calls "The Breath Release." This technique should be used several times during your workday to help eliminate the stressful thoughts and remain productive:

— Focus on the stressful situation at hand.

— Breathe in deeply and slowly. Hold it for several seconds.

— Breathe out the air as you envision all the stress leaving you.

— Repeat up to three times.

This is a very effective way to incorporate the cleansing and calming effects of mindful breathing into your work life.

Daily Practice

Here are a few suggestions for how to incorporate these points into your daily practice:

— Write and post the word "breathe" where you can see it throughout your day.

— Locate a quiet workspace area in which to reflect and practice breathing.

— Use this space to slow down, meditate, and reflect on the situation you are facing at work.

— Determine what aspect of your work takes your breath away (positively and negatively).

— Notice where you might be holding your tongue—and breath.

— Incorporate a practice of gratitude into your breathing. State an intention for which you are grateful. On the in-breath, say "thank," and on the out-breath, say "you." Repeat.

— Reflect. Write your thoughts in a journal. Breathe.

"I do my job like I breathe."
— Karl Lagerfeld

Chapter 2

STRETCH

Get out of your comfort zone.

"Do one thing every day that scares you."
— **Eleanor Roosevelt**

The Downward-Facing Dog Pose: "Adho Mukha Svanasana"

The Downward-facing Dog Pose is both energizing and restorative. This pose stretches the arms and legs, decompresses the spine, and opens the shoulders. The inversion is good for circulation and can soothe the nervous system. The pose is often seen in sun salutations, a sequence of poses designed to be done every day in the direction of the sun, typically at dawn or sunset.

HOW TO DO IT

1. **Start by kneeling with your hips stacked over your knees and your hands on the floor slightly in front of your shoulders. Point your index or middle finger forward and spread your fingers wide.**

2. **Breathe in and tuck your toes under. As you're breathing out, straighten the legs and lift your hips as high as you can. Your feet should be in line with your shoulders, your knees slightly bent, and your heels off the mat. Your weight should feel balanced between your arms and legs.**

3. **Keep your knees bent at first and work on lengthening the back, lifting your hips high. Roll the upper outer arms down toward the floor to widen the shoulders and draw your navel back toward your spine.**

4. **When you feel your back lengthen, begin to straighten your legs and lower your heels toward the mat. Do not allow your upper back to sink toward the floor. Push the mat away from you with your hands while you relax your neck. Hold this position for several breaths. On an out-breath, bring your knees back down to the mat.**

"In order to be successful, you have to be able to get out of your comfort zone, and do it often. The times that I have learned the most during my career are the times when I felt uncomfortable and had to really open my mind to a different way of working or a different point of view. Sometimes this means that you have to be willing to fail—or in other words, take a risk. It's scary. It's nerve-racking. It doesn't feel right all the time. But understanding the value of doing things differently and taking a risk is huge in being successful in not just business, but life."

— **Eric Edge**, *Manager of Global Communications, Facebook*

Stretch for Success

Stretching and getting out of your comfort zone are important parts of business success. You must take measured risks in order to learn and grow in your career. This story from Mary Kay Haben, the former president of Wm. Wrigley Jr. Company, illustrates why stretching is an important business success strategy:

"When I was about 10 years into my career (of 33 years), I was asked to do a 'non-traditional' assignment within a large 'traditional' company. The CEO asked me to be a general manager of a subsidiary company that was located in the same town but in an 'offsite' small office building. The folks working in the business were generally part of an acquired company, and so they were 'non-traditional' in their backgrounds as well. I hesitated taking the job as it was very much out of my comfort zone ... but the CEO persisted and so I accepted. Of course it was the best thing I ever did. As it was a subsidiary company, the business had a dedicated sales force, IT systems, manufacturing plants, and a full P&L. It was also a manageable size for a first time GM such as myself. (So you could take risks without concern over a 'big' impact to the total business.) I (along with my very capable team) was able to reengineer the business systems, processes, and people...and the business results followed. I loved the business and the team so much that when I was asked to move to a large, but more 'traditional' assignment ... I didn't want to go! I learned an enormous amount in that assignment and I learned to trust in those above me in terms of knowing what is best for my development, and in trying something outside of my comfort zone."

— Mary Kay Haben, *President, North America, Wm Wrigley Jr. Company (Retired)*

Here are a few tips to get you thinking outside your comfort zone and keep you stretching for more.

1."Do one thing every day that scares you." Eleanor Roosevelt famously said this, and we all remind ourselves of it on a daily basis. Whether we're networking at an industry event, brainstorming with a client, or cooking dinner for our families, we try to integrate new and different things into our daily personal and professional lives. Everyone knows that sitting comfortably at a desk while waiting for the phone to ring isn't going to bring any new, exciting clients through the door. To do that, you need to go out on a limb, be bold in promotions, and boast fairly regularly about your skills and talents. This can be quite uncomfortable for almost everyone! Still, it is a commitment to this way of thinking—stretching and moving outside of real and imagined limits—that will put you on the track to business success. By working professional muscles in new ways, you'll be able to reach for things that you couldn't envision before. This stretching allows you to push beyond your perceived professional limits in order to create the opportunities that you most want for yourself.

"I have been living WAY past my comfort zone for over a year since I started my business. BUT I have to say I never have accomplished more, been more satisfied, learned more, or have been more excited by the future. Staying in this zone has helped me to break so many barriers, mentally and spiritually. If you are stagnant, you can't learn and grow. I like being 'uncomfortable' now because I know the rewards will be great."

— Gina Duffy, *Founder & CEO SheShreds.co*

Please understand that this stretching and new way of thinking bring about their own set of challenges, similar to what happens in a gym when working with heavier weights or on a steeper incline and increased speed on the treadmill. There is a lot of huffing, puffing, and pain! Many times, you may think about giving up. But with perseverance comes the results you were searching for all along: strength and confidence in areas and in ways you didn't realize were possible.

2. Create confidence. Find your own personal ways to create confidence. If you are confident, you will be more likely to stretch and expand your universe and be successful.

"My 'safe' attire has always been a white blouse with a black skirt or pants. I decided one day my life and career needed a shift—some color perhaps? But it was going to take some confidence to make those changes and show up differently. I took the leap and began to incorporate more brightness into my attire. I aligned my essence (who I am at my core) with my attitude and what shows up to a room. I feel more like me, have more confidence and attract bolder, more vibrant clients in to my portfolio!"
— Molly Rudberg-Leshnock

3. Don't be afraid to fail. By failing, you create more opportunity. This may be counterintuitive, but it's true! As Charles Kettering said, "It is not a disgrace to fail. Failing is one of the greatest acts of the world." Take a risk, go after a dream, do something different, stretch out of your comfort zone. You may succeed or you may fail. The beauty is in how you utilize those experiences and learned ideas long into the future.

"Getting out of your comfort zone is a less-alarming way to address the subject of fear of failure, which, in my experience, is the root cause of decision paralysis. I think most of us recognize that no true learning happens in the comfort zone. By definition, if you are comfortable, you are in control of your environment … no reason to alter it through a painful learning experience by putting yourself out there. Ouch, that hurts!

With 30 years of learning experiences from some masters of the universe at delivering pain, I would like to share a simple cure. Have a mantra that becomes powerful to you in times that require moral and mental courage."

— **Donni Case, *Managing Director, Midwest, Financial Profiles, Inc.***

4. Create a personal advisory group (and include some critics). Successful companies are typically led by a diverse board of successful professionals. These are individuals from all walks of life who offer up different perspectives and experiences, which ultimately lead to a shared common goal of business success. Don't we each deserve a supportive board that focuses on what is best for us and contributes, in various ways, to the betterment of ourselves? This can be one or more individuals whom you see as mentors or advisors. Identify someone who is doing something that interests you but is beyond your current activity. Take that person out to lunch or coffee. Ask about that person's work and how he or she got to that point.

5. Do your homework. One of the best ways to "get out of your comfort zone" and stretch is to be aware of what's going on beyond your day-to-day interactions. Do research. Ask questions. It's important that you are aware of what you do and don't know. Knowing your current limitations will help you address and overcome them. Do the work. Be prepared.

"Shortly after my husband and business partner died, I was asked by a very important client to take over a project that he had been working on. A key part of that project involved me conducting a workshop for about thirty senior executives on the topic of matrix organization and how to manage within a matrix. This was not my area of expertise, so I was sweating bullets worrying about whether I would be able to deliver the high-quality product that the client expected. Since my husband had always

encouraged me to stretch myself and pursue tough goals, I took on the challenge. I worked hard to become an expert in matrix. It took a certain amount of grace under fire, willpower, and a desire to honor his memory to study my husband's books/ lectures/videos so soon after his death. He would have been proud. In the end, the client was very happy with the result and invited me to work with him again."

— Sasha Galbraith, PhD, *Partner and CFO, Jay Galbraith Management Consultants*

6. Welcome new experiences and opportunities. It is very important to business success to be open to new ideas, new ways of doing things, and new opportunities. Don't be pigeonholed as an expert in just one area. Consider moving to another city or country to get a different perspective on life and business. Take a specialized class or seminar in a new area. Be open to the possibilities that are available to you as long as you are receptive and adventurous. Make sure that the right people know that you are willing to stretch and consider a new challenge so that, when the opportunity arises, they will think of you.

"For many years I was known as a 'direct marketing expert.' It was what I was comfortable with and what I knew. I didn't have experience in other types of marketing, so I shied away from taking on those assignments. But my company was moving and expanding in different directions in order to evolve and to grow the business. And my clients were looking for a more 'holistic' approach to marketing. When we had the chance to acquire companies that specialized in promotional advertising, experiential marketing, new media, etc., my boss asked me to be in charge of merging and integrating these firms together to form a 'full-service' marketing/advertising agency. It was a major challenge but ultimately was hugely rewarding. The resulting company had great success in getting new assignments from existing clients, and winning new business from those who would not have considered working with us

before. For me personally, and professionally, it was an opportunity to stretch, grow, and achieve results that I never dreamed would be within my reach."

— Yvonne James Furth

Daily Practice

Here are a few suggestions for how to incorporate these points into your daily practice:

— Ask your direct supervisor for feedback once a month.

— Acknowledge someone for being extraordinary every day and be specific.

— Spend time in a different department and/or part of the business.

— Submit your résumé for the position you're too scared to go after.

— Sign up for a race that will challenge you physically, mentally, and emotionally.

— Create one new connection every day for thirty days.

"A mind that is stretched by a new experience can never go back to its old dimensions."

— Oliver Wendell Holmes, Jr.

Chapter 3

STRENGTH

Root yourself in a foundation of values.

*"Good actions give strength to ourselves
and inspire good actions in others."*

— **Plato**

Warrior Pose: "Virabhadrasana"

According to Richard Rosen, a contributing editor to *Yoga Journal* and director of Piedmont Yoga Studio in Oakland, California, we have to look at the metaphorical meaning of the Warrior Pose—that "the yogi is really a warrior against his own ignorance." Says Rosen, "I speculate that Virabhadrasana is about rising up out of your own limitations." This is about confronting your own limitations—emotionally, bodily, and spiritually—and finding the gaps within yourself to first acknowledge and then grow from them.

HOW TO DO IT

1. **Stand with your feet wide. Turn your left leg out ninety degrees, and turn in your right foot slightly. Your hips should be facing your left leg, with your arms out to your sides.**

2. **On an in-breath, lift your arms overhead as straight as you can with your hands together in prayer position. Drop your tailbone toward the floor and press your back heel and outer edge of your foot into the ground.**

3. **On an out-breath, lunge deeply with your left leg, keeping your knee over your ankle with your arms straight and gaze up at your palms. Breathe. Repeat with the other leg.**

"When struck with a terrible car accident, I had to reach down and find my strength to move on and pick up the pieces. I found focus and clarity and was lead to study holistic health and nutrition. I learned to live a more balanced life and became more creative and flexible to what life threw at me. Now, I'm living in the moment and enjoying every bite! If you take care of yourself, you can cultivate others and together nurture the earth."

— **Beth Aldrich, *Certified Health Counselor, Author***

Find Your Strength for Success

It is important to be strong in your convictions, rooted in your values, and firm in how you present yourself to your business and professional associates. Strength of mind and body will help you achieve your personal and professional goals, even in the midst of the most challenging situations.

Here are a few ways to find your inner strength for success:

1. Know your values. And we don't mean the ones that society or your parents expected you to hold. Doing the deep dive to discover and establish your own personal values allows you to root yourself in a foundation of meaning and credibility. Then, when anyone or anything approaches with questionable requests or ideas, you will remain steady and confident in your personal foundation and values.

"My values had been dictated by society and my parents. After some hard work and coaching, I woke up to my own personal values. I realized freedom and relationship drive who I am. Building a business around these newly discovered and voiced values changed the landscape of my business—and ultimately my client list. I've remained rooted in my values foundation and have been able to say 'no!' to a whole slew of clients and work that don't align. My work and clients finally make me happy—and vice versa."

— Molly Rudberg-Leshnock

2. Look fear in the face. With every fear faced, you grow and evolve into the successful individual you are destined to become. Growing stronger requires facing fears that, in the past, have likely stopped you cold in your tracks. From networking to cold-calling to taking financial risks, you may have heard that frightened scream in your head when asked to take a leap. We call this irrational fear the "ego." The ego wants you to stay safe, secure, and within the status quo. These messages from the ego do not allow you to evolve and learn. With a quiet mind and some meditation, you are able to hear more of your "higher self," which ultimately encourages you to step up and stand out! Your higher self realizes that, without risking and quashing your fear, you won't achieve your greatest self. By confidently stepping into fear, you prepare yourself for a journey that is uniquely yours but filled with success beyond your wildest dreams.

"Facing fears brings great opportunity!"

— **Jackie Walker Dunscomb,** *Founder and Owner of Option Dressing*

3. Remain flexible and open. Part of being strong includes knowing when to relax and let go. There will be many times when you will find yourself challenged or simply out of energy. To be strong, you must also remember to remain open to other ideas, people, energy, thoughts, opinions, and roles. Remain flexible and open in order to move fluidly through challenging relationships and work.

"I am a man of fixed and unbending principles, the first of which is to remain flexible at all times."

— **Everett Dirksen,** *former U.S. Senator*

4. Pick your battles. Every difference of opinion does not need to lead to a battle. Sometimes you have to just "let it go" if that with which you disagree doesn't affect the big picture. But on occasions when you've decided that a particular point of view is absolutely critical, then use all of your strength and energy to fight for it.

"Don't give up. The greatest obstacle to your own success is your own fear. Failure is never fun. But each time you fail, you learn something. It's often said that one should

fight to the last person standing. Hey, they're still standing! And, as a woman, I hope it's us … You have to be courageous in all that you do. You have to know when there's a time to fight."

— Sonia Sotomayor, *U.S. Supreme Court Justice*

5. Dig deep. Successful leaders are able to exert and resist great force when under pressure and to keep going against insurmountable odds. They find the strength to dig deep and garner the resolve to carry on, even when in a seemingly losing situation. They focus on giving their best and fighting hard until the end with persistent intensity and integrity throughout.

6. Always do the right thing … even when others don't. Strength of character is very important to business success. You may, from time to time, be confronted with a "questionable" situation or an ethical dilemma. Our bodies, minds, and hearts are built to recognize right from wrong. Pay attention. Choose the path that aligns with your integrity.

"Be true to yourself. It is important to commit to the things that are the most important to you as a leader. As you grow in your career and take on new responsibilities, it is inevitable that some will want you to be different things for different people. Having your core values helps you make good decisions and stay 'true to yourself.' We all have people in our lives whose 'word' doesn't hold much weight. I never wanted to be that person. In both my personal and my professional life, it is extremely important to me to stay true to my word … to be honest. If I say I'm going to do something, I do it."

— Sandy Marek, *SVP Development, Shedd Aquarium, Chicago*

7. Act decisively. Once you have a course of action planned out, be sure to act deliberately and decisively. With focus comes results. Be strong in your actions and always prepare for the unknown to show up.

"As lead board director and investor in numerous private companies as a venture capitalist, I have had to fire about four CEOs. When considering this, it is very important to gather all the facts and make the change in a deliberate manner that is well-communicated to employees; and with an interim CEO ready to step in."

— **Ellen Carnahan, *Principal, Machrie Enterprises LLC; formerly Managing Director of William Blair Capital Partners LLC***

8. Use it or lose it. Physical strength is as important as mental strength. We all know the physical benefits of strength training, including controlling weight, developing strong bones, managing chronic conditions, and boosting your stamina. In fact, the Mayo Clinic website states that the physical benefits of strength training can also sharpen your focus. Research suggests that regular strength training helps improve attention for adults.

Daily Practice

Here are a few suggestions for how to incorporate these ideas into your daily practice:

— Practice saying the bold thing daily.

— Reassess your values. Write them down in a place where you can refer back to them.

— Invest in a life coach. Through powerful dialogue, this person reflects and strengthens what you are creating in life and at work. He or she can also highlight the gaps and fears that keep you from that life.

— Hand out ten business cards every day to strangers for thirty days. Build your business muscle.

— Sign up for a mini triathlon. The swim, bike, and run will keep you working all aspects of your physical body and keep your mind on its toes.

"A person can perform only from strength ... one cannot build performance on weaknesses."
— Peter Drucker, *Author of* The Effective Executive

Chapter 4

FLEXIBILITY

Be flexible and open to new ideas.

"The willow is my favorite tree. I grew up near one. It's the most flexible tree in nature and nothing can break it—no wind, no elements, it can bend and withstand anything."

— Pink, *Entertainer*

Triangle Pose: "Trikonasana"

The Triangle Pose helps to align the hips, legs, and torso. It also helps to develop strength, flexibility, and stamina.

HOW TO DO IT

1. Begin by standing with your feet three to four feet apart. Breathe in.

2. Raise your arms up to your shoulders with palms facing down. Lift your thighs and knee caps. Broaden your chest and lengthen your back.

3. Turn your left foot out ninety degrees to your body by turning your left leg out directly from the hip socket.

4. Turn the toes of your right foot slightly in.

5. On an out-breath, fold deeply into your left hip socket. Lengthen your body to your left side. Put your left hand on your left ankle or shin (or the floor), raising your right arm straight to the ceiling. Keep your gaze up at your hand. Repeat on the other side.

"The ability to be flexible may be the most underrated yet most essential characteristic of a successful leader. What we learn as we develop and oversee people, departments, and companies is that obstacles will come our way that will try to take us off course. It is the responsibility of a good leader to find other avenues and remain flexible in order to achieve success. Each day brings us a new and unexpected challenge. We need to view these challenges as opportunities. I was given an opportunity to create a department with young, motivated individuals that I would not have otherwise had the privilege to have met, mentor, and call my friends. The opportunity of a lifetime was given to me. I would not have enjoyed its success without learning to be flexible."

— **Christine McCarthy,** *former Sr. Director of Claims and Litigation, Northshore University Health System (previously Evanston Northwestern Healthcare)*

Be Flexible for Success

Flexibility is often key to successful business practice. It is important to be able to look at a problem or a situation from all sides. Evaluate all options. Be flexible in how you approach the potential solution and open yourself up to view these solutions through numerous lenses.

1. Think unconventionally. If you always approach a situation in the same way, the outcome isn't likely to vary much. You won't be as innovative or creative as you could be. One of the keys to business success is thinking differently. (Remember Apple?)

"Mario Andretti famously said 'If everything is under control, you aren't going fast enough.' Never has this metaphor been more apt in business than it is today. If we are comfortable and working within parameters with which we are very familiar, we must not be pushing new thinking enough. The pace of change in business and in marketing is so fast that only by stretching our minds and learning something new do we have a hope of staying relevant. Flexibility and a willingness to try the uncomfortable will define the executive of the 21st Century."

— Nick Jones, *EVP, Retail Practice Lead, Leo Burnett/ARC*

2. Listen to other points of view. Don't be too rigid in your conviction that your way is the only way to get something done. Be open to other ways to approach a situation. Look at the problem or issue from all sides. Seek out other peoples' opinion and listen to their points of view.

3. Don't be afraid to change your mind. True business intelligence comes from growing and expanding how you approach an issue. Even if you've strongly stated a position one way, it's OK to change your mind in light of new information or further thought.

"Flexibility is a key success factor in business (and life!). My personal philosophy is that you can never make a mistake, so you might as well keep moving! A mistake is only an unplanned learning opportunity so you garner what you need to know and adjust.

"Nothing ever goes exactly as planned, and most failures are caused by sticking to the plan regardless of whether or not it's working. By being flexible you can flow with any situation and make room for the best outcome given the circumstances.

"It's important to remain flexible to identify and take advantage of opportunities as well. Success requires you to be mindful of the landscape at all times. A plan usually only represents your best guess at the time, based on the information you have. As you gain more information and insight, flexibility allows you to accommodate new learnings and make the most of any situation."

— **Dorri McWhorter, *CEO, YWCA Chicago***

4. Embrace change. Don't be afraid of change. You need to take some risks in order to be great. Just because you used to do something one way doesn't mean it's the only way. Change. Evolve. Grow.

"I had been laid off from a law firm that was downsizing significantly on its way to shuttering altogether. I was interested in moving to Dallas, but was VERY interested in the in-house position in Chicago. I agreed to be flexible about my location to get the opportunity I really wanted—the in-house counsel job with MCI. I decided that being flexible about this would serve my long-term career interests. We agreed that I would train for a short time in Chicago, then move. I had an office and an admin in Dallas, and a target date for relocation. The stars aligned, though, as shortly after I took the job, the announced merger between British Telecom and MCI was

abruptly called off. In light of the resulting uncertainty, MCI decided to keep me in Chicago indefinitely rather than requiring me to relocate. By the time the dust had settled and the company made plans for its (ill-fated) merger with WorldCom, I had demonstrated an ability to serve my Dallas clients just fine from Chicago, and they never required me to move. But if I hadn't been flexible about that possibility, I would have missed a great opportunity that ultimately led to my current job, in Chicago, which I love!"

— **Kathleen Myalls,** *Legal Counsel, The Interpublic Group of Companies*

5. See the bigger picture. Look at your situation in the broader context. If you consider the bigger picture, you will be better able to see possible ways to approach your problem or situation. Always keep the big picture in mind and don't sweat the small stuff.

6. Wear many different hats. We are often called upon to do many different tasks—sometimes at the same time. Remain flexible and poised as you take on each of these roles.

"I currently am micro-managing and getting involved in all facets of publishing: sales, editorial, art direction, conceptualization of photography, feature stories, and illustration. As a small business owner, cash flow, accounting, purchasing, and legal issues also come into play on a regular basis."

— **Sherren Leigh,** *President/Publisher,* TCW Magazine (Today's Chicago Woman)

7. Bend without breaking. Being able to let go and adapt to change is an important asset in your work life. Fast Company rates flexibility as the number one characteristic of a great leader. When things don't go as originally planned, be open to course-correcting toward a plan B. Good leaders have the ability to absorb the unexpected and remain flexible, not defensive. Just like a quarterback during a broken play, a good leader must often look at all options and decide quickly on a new course of action.

"Nearly every company where I've worked has had constant organizational changes. They say the only constant is change. If you want to succeed in this environment, you need to prove that you can be flexible and adapt to changes such as new roles, new priorities and new leadership."

— Kim Schubeck, *Director of Naturals, The Scotts Miracle-Gro Company*

8. Be stubborn and flexible. Jeff Bezos, founder and CEO of Amazon says, "We are stubborn on vision. We are flexible on details. If you're not stubborn, you'll give up on experiments too soon. And if you're not flexible, you'll pound your head against the wall and you won't see a different solution to a problem you're trying to solve." The challenge is in knowing when to be flexible and when to stick to your vision.

Daily Practice

Here are a few suggestions for how to incorporate these ideas into your daily practice:

— Sign up for an improv class. Improv takes us in to the unknown, challenging us to go with the flow while keeping our minds sharp.

— Start a mastermind group in your organization focused only on brainstorming and unconventional thinking.

— Surround yourself and your team with bendable, vibrant toys. Bring them to meetings. Think of these things as the people and ideas in your business.

— Practice flexibility in conversation, at the gym, with family, and with work projects.

"I learned to always take on things I'd never done before. Growth and comfort do not coexist."

—**Virginia Rometty, *CEO, IBM***

Chapter 5

GRACE

Handle yourself with grace and good humor.

"The ideal man bears the accidents of life with dignity and grace, making the best of circumstances."

— Aristotle

Lord of the Dance Pose: "Natarajasana"

The Lord of the Dance Pose (or the Dancer's Pose) is considered a "standing posture." It is one of the poses that strengthens leg muscles and joints, keeps the spine flexible and long, opens the heart, and increases circulation to the lower extremities.

HOW TO DO IT

1. **Stand straight with your feet together and your big toes touching. As you inhale, shift your weight onto your right foot.**

2. **Lift your left heel toward your left buttock as you bend the knee. Keep the standing leg straight and strong. Keep your torso as upright as you can.**

3. **Reach back with your left hand and grasp the outside of your left foot or ankle.**

4. **Lift your left foot up and back, away from your torso. Stretch your right arm forward, parallel to the floor. Release gently and repeat on the other leg.**

"Without humor, nothing else matters. Humor provides balance and strength to me in this crazy business."

— **Kary McIlwain,** *President, North American Managing Partner, Y&R Advertising*

Be Gracious for Success

Successful business professionals will tell you that, in order to succeed, you must handle each situation or challenge with grace. Nice girls do, in fact, get the corner office. Grace is another term for good humor, calmness, integrity, and having a generally pleasant demeanor—all characteristics of a successful business leader.

"The advertising business is one in which women tend to excel. It's often described as a 'female-friendly' industry. That usually is meant as shorthand for a 'service-oriented' business. Whether it's because we handle stress more gracefully, demonstrate more compassion, have a higher EQ, or are just more willing to suck it up and get on with it, women historically have done well in advertising. I recently experienced one of the great lessons of my career—one of those 'teachable moments' people always talk about. In working with a new colleague, I found us disconcertingly at odds on nearly everything. He delivered very direct criticism on my performance, but in the most general terms. It hurt like hell, but I had to probe for specifics.

"His issues with me were with the 'female aspects' of my performance. I was a 'consensus-builder.' I was 'too friendly' with the staff. People wouldn't 'follow me into war.' This is a common metaphor for leadership, this 'following someone into war' thing. It's a fundamentally male concept. I suppose it's easy to forget that in every war (real or metaphorical), women fought, and led, and were followed—but because people chose to follow them, not because a leader commanded them to do so. I came away from this experience better in some ways—at least in terms of understanding that others' expectations of you aren't necessarily perfectly valid,

but … they're worth provoking a good, honest, self-assessment. I'll be a better CEO because of the lessons someone taught me. In his effort to make the essence of 'me' (read: woman) seem weak, he made me stronger in my determination to be a leader people will choose to follow."

— **Kristi VandenBosch,** *Chief Digital Officer, Meredith Xcelerated Marketing*

1. Find your North Star and stick with it. It's often "easier" to go with the majority in any given situation. Make your own determination as to what is the right thing to do and do it, even if it is different or challenging to others. Trust your intuition. Listen to your gut.

"Integrity is the most important element in character. I live and breathe it in my personal as well as my professional life. I firmly believe in everything it stands for and how it plays an intricate part in my life."

— **Delena D. Spann,** *Fraud Analysis & White-Collar Crime Expert, U.S. Government Agency and/or U.S. Federal Law Enforcement Agency*

Sometimes you have to do the right thing, even if you aren't sure that it's necessarily "best for business." In the long run, it may prove to be best for everyone.

"My company, ChoiceCare, changed the financing and delivery of healthcare in Cincinnati, knowing we would become a target of our competitors and suppliers. Regardless, it was the right thing to do for the community and future of our industry. Through a change in management process that included all stakeholders, we drove this change that ultimately captured market leading quality scores and market share."

— **Jane Rollinson,** *Former President and CEO, ChoiceCare, and Coauthor of* The Rower's Code

2. Keep your sense of humor. It's important not to take yourself—and the situation—too seriously. If something goes wrong, try to be good-humored about it and turn the situation around without animosity. Remember the joy that's inherent in the job that you are doing and embrace it. Have fun! Be friendly and have a positive outlook. You'll be surprised at how infectious this type of attitude can be.

"I've lost new business pitches, and rather than get angry or abusive, I've been supportive and graceful. A couple of times this has led to assignments later on from the same clients who cited our 'grace' as the reason they came back to us. Good manners, grace, and a smile go a long way in this business."
— **Tony Weisman,** *CEO, DigitasLBi/NA*

3. Give credit where credit is due. Be sure to commend your colleagues for a job well done and give credit for the work to the team or the individuals who helped to achieve this.

"Once when I was traveling on my own to give a new business pitch, I won the account and called my team back at the office to give them the good news. Then I called my boss from the airport to tell him. He said, 'Great job, and you did it on your own.' I immediately said, 'Thank you, but it was really the whole creative and new business team back at the office that deserves the credit. They set me up for success.' He said 'That's why you're such a good leader.'"
— **Yvonne James Furth**

4. Take a compliment. Learning how to just say "thank you" when someone tells you something positive or gives you a compliment is important. Don't denigrate the work you've done or shy away from such praise in an attempt to be humble. On the other hand, never brag about your successes inappropriately.

"When people like you, they assume you know what you're doing and often give you the benefit of the doubt in situations."

— **Angela Elbert,** *Partner, Neal Gerber Eisenberg*

5. Be a good listener. It's important to hear all sides of any story before you make a decision and to take a healthy interest in the people whom you work with. Be open and honest, and listen to your coworkers. A good idea can come from anywhere or anyone. You just have to be open to it. Sometimes listening can be a very effective leadership tool.

"In one specific situation, I needed to vie for authority against a male creative counterpart. To do so, I needed to show strength of character and vision that was more thoughtful and impactful than his so the team would choose to follow my directions. I used grace and good humor to win the hearts of the team, while being strong in words and in stature so I was a person worth following. I also showed flexibility in listening and bending with input from the team so they saw how they could be part of the process moving forward. Needless to say, they were quickly swayed."

— **Heidi Schoeneck,** *EVP, Creative Director, Geometry Global*

6. Be generous with your words and with your time. Giving back to your community and to your industry is a very important part of being successful. You've heard the saying that, "in giving back, you get much more than you give." That's so true.

"The personal satisfaction I get from my work with the Off The Street Club kids is amazing. It's really not just about giving my time, but about the wonderful feeling of satisfaction and good will that I get from each encounter. The added benefit of my work with this well-deserving cause is all the camaraderie and friendship that I

have gained—not to mention the wealth of people who are now in my personal and professional network. I wouldn't have met these people without it."

— Yvonne James Furth

7. Keep calm and carry on. Always remain calm, even in the face of chaos. Be a calming force that inspires confidence among your colleagues. It's very important for business leaders not to panic.

"When a crisis hits, a strong leader must remain steadfast and calm. I have seen this over and over in my career. The leaders who overreact, or begin to yell and panic, generally do not do the right thing for the company or the individuals. They tend to make poor decisions and rush to judgement. The worst thing a leader can do is assume the worst and behave that way. People look for strong, calm leadership in a crisis. When the stock market crashed in 2008, I watched leaders panic and I watched our leaders not panic. They looked at the opportunity that lied ahead. They took their time to develop a strategy that was longer term in focus and would enable the company to flourish."

— Suzy Domenick, *VP, Human Resources, Prudential Annuities*

A focus on grace, dignity, and humaneness is not a new issue. In fact, B. C. Forbes founded *Forbes Magazine* in 1917 to help inspire greater humaneness in business. Cadbury and Clarke's are two companies founded on "right" principles.

Daily Practice

Here are a few suggestions on how to incorporate these ideas into your daily practice:

— Create a gratitude habit. First thing in the morning, thank someone via e-mail, text, or personally.

— Create an "Out of Integrity" list. Write down some of the things in your life and work that you feel are not aligned with your values. Cross off one item each day.

— Watch the movie *Ghandi.* Notice how, even in times of sorrow, pain, and challenge, Ghandi shows humor, generosity, and grace.

— Smile. It's contagious.

"Courage is grace under pressure."
— **Ernest Hemingway**

Chapter 6

ENDURANCE

Prepare and plan for the long haul.

"*Most of the important things in the world have been accomplished by people who have kept on trying when there seemed to be no hope at all.*"

— **Dale Carnegie,** *Author*

The Bridge Pose: "Setu Bandhasana"

According to *SHAPE* magazine, the Bridge Pose is a gentle inversion that works with gravity to open your entire chest and shoulder area. Because the chest is lifted up toward the chin, your thyroid gland is impacted and massaged. The thyroid makes the hormones that regulate metabolism.

HOW TO DO IT

1. **Lie on your back with your knees bent and feet hip-distance apart and parallel. On an out-breath, pull up your pelvis and abdomen, lifting your hips off the floor.**

2. **Put your hands together underneath the small of your back, linking your fingers. Bring your shoulder blades together, raising your body as high as you can without putting any strain on the back of your neck. Open your chest and breathe for a few seconds.**

"Endurance and flexibility are indispensable if you are going to start a business. It requires a lot of time and energy and you need to adjust quickly to changing conditions."

— **Taryn Rose, *MD, CEO, DRESR, LLC***

Build Endurance for Success

We've all been tested in our work. We're compelled to not only create but to complete—to remain confident and strong in achieving our end goal. Achieving this end requires endurance—the patience, persistence, and focus to stay the course.

Most of us strive to deliver excellence in our daily work without much intention or thought. We lock and load, envision the end result, strive for the very best outcomes, and hope the day will come when our project is complete. Then we celebrate!

Unfortunately, most of our celebrations come with a price. Never before have we been such an unhealthy tribe, with cancer, heart disease, autoimmune disorders, allergies, etc.—not to mention fatigue and obesity! We are an excellent bunch of professionals delivering on expectations, but we're paying a very steep price with our bodies, minds, and hearts.

Yet, some individuals sail through the work and celebrate their success without regret and with healthy habits and a clear mind. Gone are the days when we'll sacrifice ourselves for our successes. You can endure and prosper through your career with a healthy mind, body, and spirit. We recognize and are committed to a more expansive view of the professional world. We're looking for professionals who are willing to engage in this new approach, endure, and succeed.

What can you do to commit to the long haul?

1. Fill your cup. Imagine yourself as a cup filled with energy and lightness. How successful you are in both work and life depends on your dedication to filling that cup—as well as how often it is drained. A cup that is well cared for, filled with vitality and health, and regulated is a cup that will endure over time. Individuals who tend to their personal cups find that, despite the demands placed upon them, they last and thrive. Filling your cup requires gratitude, self-care, connecting with loved ones, working toward and achieving a goal, and healthy celebrations. Review your cup regularly.

2. Seek support. Sometimes we need help in order to "stick with it" and achieve our goals. Be willing to hire a coach or find a mentor to guide you through challenging times. Be willing to accept support from your family, friends, and network when and if needed.

"I was randomly going to the gym during the week and chaotically choosing different strength training machines and cardio exercises. Even with all of this, none of my personal fitness goals were being reached. I questioned my commitment, my process, and finally my passion for the hard work.

— What was missing?

— Why was I working so hard?

— What WAS my goal anyway? Maybe I should quit this all together!

"I needed guidance. So I enlisted the support of a personal trainer—someone who could encourage me when I felt like running away. To endure, we must enlist the help of others who can see things much more clearly and support us in ways in which we cannot support ourselves. After hiring a personal trainer, I tackled numerous running races, triathlons, and finally, two half-ironmans. He helped me set goals, was a partner in the pain along the way, and celebrated the successes as I went along."

— Molly Rudberg-Leshnock

3. Create healthy habits. Continue to show up and do the work. Sooner or later, you won't notice that you're lifting/bending/pushing more weight or accomplishing more than you could have imagined. Set goals and work up to them in manageable increments. It doesn't take too long to forge good habits. After the initial investment, they require very little energy. A 2009 study at University College London determined that it can take as little as sixty-six days for a behavior to become automatic.

> *"Starting a business is like being at the beginning of a marathon … any number of things can go wrong, despite training, and you need to make sure that you deal quickly with any unexpected issues that come along the way. In my case, the issues came almost immediately … investors termed it a 'babysitters club' and said things like 'my wife handles that.' I spent years pounding phones, flyer-ing on foot, and talking to anyone that would listen to build the beta site. And then … that's when the real race began. I find that anytime you get the chance to sit back and rest, something is wrong. You should always be pushing, moving, chasing."*
>
> **— Genevieve Thiers,** *Founder and Former CEO, Sittercity.com*

4. Commit and see it through. Business success is a marathon, not a sprint. You often have to hang in there through the tough times in order to reap the benefits during the productive periods.

> *"True success is not short-term achievement. You can be lucky once, but to be really successful requires a high level of effort over a long period of time. My father often told us that we should be frugal in our business so that we can last another day. That last day might be the day you get a big contract or something else happens to allow you to continue on."*
>
> **— Nik Rokop,** *Industry Assistant Professor of Entrepreneurship,*
> *Stuart School of Business, Illinois Institute of Technology*

5. Rest. Sometimes you have to rest for success.

"Physical health (strength, sleep, balance) play a role in my success every day. When I am tired or not feeling well, I am unable to properly plan, react, and think. I used to believe that I was 'too busy' to take the time to exercise, until I realized the company needed me to be at peak energy and health. Giving myself 'permission' to take healthy steps has made all the difference in my ability to stay healthy and be successful."

—Karen Sauder, *Industry Director, Google*

How we function daily—as well as how we age—is a symptom of how much rest we allow ourselves. Studies have shown that, without rest, we lack focus and strength and cannot bring our best work to light. Hard work requires a reprieve from time to time, and research shows we're simply not getting enough of it. According to the National Sleep Foundation, adults need seven to nine hours of sleep every night, yet approximately 30 percent of adults reported an average of less than six hours of sleep per night. This has a huge impact on the bottom line and the quality of our work! Carve out time in your day to not only meditate and reflect, but to settle your mind, body, and heart as well. Without this intention, your work, as well as your immune system, will suffer. May Sarton writes, "The most valuable thing we can do for the psyche, occasionally, is to let it rest, wander, live in the changing light of room, not try to be or do anything whatever." To fill our cup, we need to create the energy and space to do just that—fill and drain ourselves thoughtfully … and endure. With rest comes revitalization and energy for the long haul.

Daily Practice

Here are a few ideas on how to incorporate these suggestions into your daily practice:

— Take a twenty-minute nap during lunch.

— Start each day with thirty minutes of movement.

— Meditate for five minutes in the corner of your office for thirty days.

— Take a leisurely walk in the sun to get centered and quiet your mind.

— Take a "well-being day" off from work in order to get revitalized.

— Find the areas of your life that consistently weigh you down. Ask for support.

— Commit to seven to nine hours of sleep each night.

"Excellence is not a singular act, but a habit.
You are what you repeatedly do."
—Shaquille O'Neill, *NBA, Celebrity*

Chapter 7

FOCUS

Stay focused on the task at hand.

"The shorter way to do many things is to do only one thing at a time."

—Mozart

Eagle Pose: "Garudasana"

The Eagle Pose focuses your energy at Ajna Chakra, which lies above and between your eyes, thereby focusing your attention inward. It stretches the muscles across your shoulders and upper back, helping to release tension in these areas. This posture is especially helpful if you sit at a desk or computer for several hours per day.

HOW TO DO IT

1. **Stand with your feet hip-distance apart. Raise your arms to shoulder height on an in-breath.**

2. **On an out-breath, bend your knees, going as low as you can without lifting your heels. Then cross your left leg over your right knee. Tuck your left foot behind your right calf.**

3. **Keep your hips level and legs bent. Cross your right arm over your left, with palms facing up. Bend the elbows, bringing your hands together.**

4. **Lift your arms straight up as far as you can. Breathe steadily and close your eyes, focusing on the Ajna Chakra. Repeat with your legs and arms in the opposite direction.**

"I think that focus is key to business success, especially for women. We have so many things pulling us in different directions (work, family, community) and, because we are master multitaskers, we often try to do it all. I learned the power of focus when I joined Walmart several years ago. I commuted from Dallas to Bentonville for the first year so that my daughter could finish her senior year of high school. While it was hard to be away from my family, when I was in Bentonville, I was able to completely focus on work (a blessing when you are starting a new job). And when I was home, I was singularly focused on my husband, daughter, and son (even more of a blessing). I've tried to remember that you really can do it all, just not all at the same time."

— **Cindy Davis,** *EVP, Global Customer Insights, Walmart*

Focus for Success

Staying focused is critical to business success. It is especially important in today's hectic lives, where you are pulled in many different directions at the same time. Success requires you to focus on the task at hand and give it your full attention, then you can move on to the next challenge with an equal amount of focus. To borrow a saying from a high school football coach, it's about "W.I.N.—What's Important Now." If you focus on what's important right now, then you will be a winner. Of course we can all prioritize what's most important in our lives (family, health, faith, etc.) in whatever order we like. However, there are times when you have to put those thoughts aside while you concentrate on getting your work done. That's not to say that those priorities are any less important; it just means that you need to focus your attention on the assignment or job of that moment.

1. Set realistic goals. Don't put yourself in a losing situation by setting unrealistic goals. Know what you can and cannot achieve in any given time period. Make a list and put together a plan to get it done. If you are trying to do too much, you will never be able to focus or succeed.

2. Schedule your time appropriately. Be sure that you have allowed enough time in your daily or weekly schedule to get everything done. If you are frantically trying to bake cookies for your daughter's fundraiser while you are getting ready to go to work and reviewing the presentation you have to give today, you will be too stressed to get any of it done (or at least done well). Bake the cookies the night before and take the time to have breakfast with your kids in the morning before you all head to work and school.

"Whenever I do anything, I like to give it my all. I'm a big believer in 'work at work' and 'home at home.' I always have tried very hard to draw a hard line between work life and home life. I think it's very important to be completely available for

your family when you are at home and not distracted by work issues. It is equally important that you are not worried about what's going on at home or distracted while you are at work."

— Yvonne James Furth

3. Clear your desk or workspace. Be sure to move away anything that might distract you from your task. Only surround yourself with the tools you need to get the job done. Create an environment where you can focus and not be distracted. If you work at home, be sure to have a separate room or office where you can have the space and solitude to get your work done. If you focus better in a quiet environment, make sure that there are no distractions around you. Some people prefer to work with soft music playing in the background. Figure out what works best for you and set up your environment for success.

4. Prioritize your tasks. Avoid getting overwhelmed by the many tasks that you have to accomplish. Focus on just those few things that will really make a difference. Don't get distracted by the unimportant things that don't contribute to your success or that of your business. Don't sweat the small stuff.

"Running a thriving coaching business, writing a book, raising two boys, working out, connecting with my husband, continuing my education, spending quality time with friends, being of service to organizations I deeply care for. These are my daily commitments and what bring me joy. In order to bring calm to the potential chaos, I begin every day with a Top 6 priority list and do not waver from it. It keeps me present, grounded and aligned with my commitments and passions in life."

— Molly Rudberg-Leshnock

5. Don't multitask. That seems impossible in today's world, right? But Douglas Merrill (former CIO of Google) says that multitasking interferes with your brain's ability to perform at peak capacity. Do one thing at a time and give it your best effort instead of existing somewhere in between all of your roles. Utilize intention and focus.

Daily Practice

Here are a few suggestions for how you can incorporate these ideas into your daily practice:

— Hire a professional organizer, a person trained to bring a new level of efficiency to your life. One good resource for this is the National Association of Professional Organizers (www.napo.net). Do it now.

— Plan tomorrow today. Every night, take ten minutes to plan out your next day.

— Write up, post, and notice your "Distraction List." Be aware of what distracts you from your "plan tomorrow today" list. Choose differently.

— Notice when you aren't focused on the now.

— Commit to collecting twenty new business cards per week. Focus on generating connections and leads.

"Do the hard jobs first. The easy jobs will take care of themselves."
— **Dale Carnegie,** *Author*

Chapter 8

BALANCE

Carve out balance in your life.

"The best and safest thing is to keep a balance in your life, acknowledge the great powers around us and in us. If you can do that, and live that way, you are really a wise man."

— **Euripides, *Ancient Greek Writer and Philosopher***

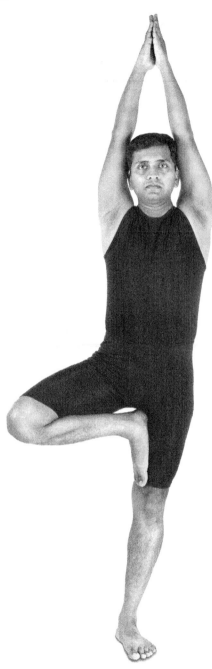

Tree Pose: "Vrksasana"

The Tree Pose is extremely beneficial in helping to maintain physical and mental equilibrium. Balance is sometimes affected by your emotional state. You can learn to calm your mind by learning to balance your body.

HOW TO DO IT

1. **Start by standing with your feet parallel and slightly apart. Make sure to equally distribute your weight between both feet. Transfer your weight onto your left foot.**

2. **Lengthen your lower back and engage your abdominal muscles. Place the sole of your right foot on your left inner calf or thigh. (Do not rest your foot on your knee, but place it directly above or below.)**

3. **Turn your right knee out by ninety degrees. Put your hands together in a prayer pose in front of your chest or raise your arms straight above your head. Keep your left leg straight and strong.**

4. **Focus your attention on an object in front of you to help you keep your balance. Breathe. Repeat on the other side.**

"Above all, balance is essential as it is a grounding that is necessary for success. I often say there is a minor change to go from iNbalance to iMbalance; however these minor changes can make a significant impact on one's life. It is the day-to-day decisions we make, however minor, that determine our overall balance. One by itself may not seem significant, but add them up and it is the difference between an OK life and a great life."

— **Jean Kolb, *Director of Wellness, The Kohler Company***

Balance for Success

Prioritize your life and work to make the most of each day. You can "have it all," just not all at the same time. Your spiritual center should always be your measure of success. This chapter addresses the importance of successfully balancing work, life, and service.

Balance is more than just a "buzzword." With balance, you can reach the corner office and still be able to enjoy your life outside of work. Opportunities are plentiful for you to carve out balance in your life. Here are a few lessons learned regarding life-work balance to help you achieve your balance.

1. Work hard and smart. An unshakable work ethic is critical for success. Anything is possible if you set your mind to it. Make the most of your day in order to stay as productive as possible. Minimize meetings if you can. Only say "yes" to those projects and meetings that focus on your goals. Say "no" more often.

2. Stay focused. With only twenty-four hours in a day, and modern technology keeping us connected constantly, it's important to balance time at home with time at work. When home, focus 100 percent of your time there. When working, focus 100 percent on the work. Set boundaries and stick to them. Obviously there will be times when unexpected things arise. This is when we call on flexibility.

3. Nurture friendships. Friends are very important and provide yet another aspect of balance in life. Gather your friends, like flowers, from the various important parts of your life: high school, college, community, and work. Guard and nurture these friendships dearly. They provide a balance and grounding that is invaluable.

4. Respect family. Family is a very important part of your life whether or not you are married or have any living parents or siblings. Your family grounds you and provides a foundation for being at peace as well as for being successful in your life.

"I married my high school sweetheart over thirty years ago. And while I was working my way up the corporate ladder, he was building a successful law practice. But as two working professionals we kept each other grounded and focused on the importance of family, which includes our two sons. Our balanced partnership is based on love and respect, and we've transferred that respect to our sons, who will take into their lives a healthy appreciation for working mothers, working fathers, and the challenge of balancing both."

— Yvonne James Furth

5. Calibrate time. When at work, strive to carefully calibrate your time at the office, making sure to give the right amount of attention to clients and staff. Both are important and both deserve the appropriate amount of time. Additionally, both can challenge you as well as teach you about collaboration and the true meaning of partnership. Balancing both well can power your personal success as well as that of your business. This balance can lead you to the corner office.

6. Build resources. Another good way to create balance is to surround yourself with excellent resources. Hire great people, then stand back and let them do their jobs. Surround yourself with people who are the best and brightest in the business as well as outside of it. In the same way that you utilize resources to be efficient at work, consider resources that will allow you to do the same at home.

7. Experience life. Oftentimes, work can be all-consuming. You may spend every waking minute there, not to mention sleepless nights, if you allow your life to be defined by your job. Consider this: How can you expect to do your job well if you don't personally witness what makes the world work? Without question, there are times when you may have to work long nights and weekends. But that should be the exception, not the rule, in any business. Travel. See the world. Experience life! In doing so, you will increase your balance, and your expanded perspective will be invaluable to your business.

> *"In my work with Global Volunteers, I've often been awestruck in the midst of an important community event—such as a funeral or graduation—when I look around and I might be one of the only 'outsiders' who may be engaged in the event. I think to myself what a privilege it is to be accepted into this community and to share such personal moments. I'm humbled. I'm left breathless. When a mother cries and says over and over 'thank you, thank you, you're my angel.' Or a shy preschooler pats my face and says 'mi amigo.' I can't measure the restorative impact this has on my psyche. It's like medicine. Or a good night's sleep."*
>
> **— Michele Gran, *Cofounder, SVP, Global Volunteers***

8. Mentor. In addition to seeking balance in the office, take a look at serving others and the ways in which that can enrich and fulfill you so that you can continue working and living as joyfully as possible. It is very gratifying to be able to further other young men's and women's careers. Be confident and share your story with those who can benefit from your experience. Be a leader. Lead by example. Show those who are "up and coming" what it takes to be successful.

> *"The more women help one another, the more we help ourselves. Acting like a coalition truly does produce results. … Any coalition of support must also include men, many of whom care about gender inequality as much as women do."*
>
> **— Sheryl Sandberg, *COO Facebook, Author,* Lean In: Women, Work and the Will to Lead**

9. Have fun. Whoever said that all work and no play makes for a dull company was dead on. Work hard; play hard. Help to create a special, balanced environment at your company—one where people actually look forward to coming to work each day. Take on the same mind-set outside of your work life.

10. Give back. Life cannot be all about work. Your clients are the lifeblood of your business, and the employees are the heart. But you cannot afford to insulate yourself to the extent that you lose sight of your soul. That is why giving back to the community is very much a part of the culture of balance. Many busy professional people have devoted countless hours to helping charities in need, which creates a healthier and more well-rounded workforce. And, ultimately, this practice helps to keep your perspective. It is true that you get back far more than you give.

> "In my work as a Global Volunteer, I've felt this 'communion' between people of divergent cultures. It seems to be magnified by the intensity of the work project. It's as if the tower of life's difficulties collapses and the moment is expanded to accommodate a rare clarity of human commonality. How do you describe that? It's so satisfying, it becomes a hunger, really, over the years. Funny how as I've grown older, I've become more hungry for these true 'authentic' moments with people. While the hands-on work we do is absolutely crucial to most of our host partners, the real magic occurs in these random, spiritual moments of interpersonal communion.
>
> "I think that's what happens during yoga practice. The goal for me is to provide space in my life—in my mind—for that connection with the energy of the universe which unites us all. It happens to me on almost every Global Volunteers service program in a different way. Just as yoga manipulates my body and breath to raise my consciousness, working on a common project with people in a selfless way raises me to a different plane of existence. Careful, lest it become addictive!"
>
> **— Michele Gran, *Cofounder, SVP, Global Volunteers***

Daily Practice

Here are a few suggestions on how to incorporate these ideas into your daily practice:

— Identify the top six things in your life that fulfill you. Write them down, post them, and take action on the list.

— Create a well-being checklist. Look at not just the physical well-being of your life but also at the spiritual, emotional, and mental aspects. How are these being cared for and supported?

— Go through your calendar for the next seven days. Remove the items that do not support your commitment to a balanced life.

— Find someone who needs mentoring and take them out to lunch. Invest your time in that person and check in on him or her periodically.

— Commit to a date night with your partner or a friend. Invest in fun and play.

— Volunteer for a cause that interests you. Do this regularly.

— Travel to a place that you've never dreamed of visiting.

— Play with balance. Everyone has a different equilibrium.

"If you are interested in 'balancing' work and pleasure, stop trying to balance them. Instead make your work more pleasurable."

—Donald Trump, *Businessman, Celebrity*

Chapter 9

MEDITATION

Breathe and let go.

"I've been meditating for years. I haven't missed a day since
the day I started … It's the equivalent of a couple of hours more sleep."

—George Stephanopoulos, *TV Journalist*

Corpse Pose: "Savasana"

Meditation is a quiet time when our body and mind connect to commune with our higher self and the work we do in our lives.

. . . .

HOW TO DO IT

1. Prepare your mind and body to relax for at least ten minutes. Don't think about your to-do list or what groceries you need to buy.

2. Lie comfortably on your back with your feet slightly apart, letting your legs open comfortably. Close your eyes. Put a towel over your eyes to help you relax deeply without light or other distractions.

3. Relax all of your muscles. Keep your palms up and your arms slightly away from your body. Visualize each part of your body, relaxing one part at a time.

4. Your breath should be soft and steady. Direct your breath to any areas in your body where you feel any tension to help you relax completely. Rest for ten minutes or more.

5. When you are ready to come out of this pose, slowly bring your arms over your head to stretch gently. Bend your knees and roll to your right side. Slowly rise to a sitting position.

. . . .

"Meditation has improved my ability to listen and think creatively. It has had a clear, positive impact on my business and client relationships."

—**Gina Marotta,** ***Happiness and Life Coach, Former Managing Director of StepUp Women's Network in Chicago***

Meditate for Success

Taking the time to reflect on what you are doing in the moment is an essential part of achieving a healthy mind, body, and spirit. It's important to clear your mind so that you can address the challenges as they come your way with clarity, peace, and a fresh outlook.

Scientific evidence has shown that the brain functioning of serious meditators is overwhelmingly different from that of nonmeditators. It differs in ways that suggested an increased capacity to focus and handle emotions. As illustrated in the 2009 study with the descriptive title, "Long Term Meditation Is Associated With Increased Gray Matter Density In The Brain Stem," neuroscientists used MRIs to compare the brains of meditators with nonmeditators. The structural differences observed led the scientists to speculate that certain benefits, like improved cognitive, emotional and immune responses, can be tied to this growth and its positive effects on breathing and heart rate (cardiorespiratory control).

Meditation, therefore, is a kind of mental exercise that remains essential and powerfully enhances how you approach and do business.

1. Commit to twenty minutes of quiet each day. In our smartphone-infested working world, taking the time to disconnect and focus on your higher self can be a challenge; the practice is even questioned by some. But, increasingly, hardworking professionals are doing what it takes to help them thrive in their lives. This includes at least ten to thirty minutes of quiet each day whenever one can find the time. By quieting your mind and body, you become more aware of your intentions, hopes, fears, and desires. You are also better able to focus on getting the job done.

Oprah Winfrey is a strong advocate of meditation—sometimes twice a day. After one such session, she said: "I walked away feeling fuller than when I'd come in—full of hope, a sense of contentment, and deep joy. Knowing for sure that even in the daily craziness that bombards us from every direction, there is—still—the constancy of stillness. Only from that can you create your best work and your best life."

"The biggest benefit from my yoga practice is the ability to quiet my mind. It seems paradoxical that exerting oneself through yoga and meditation would create prosperity in work, but it does."

— Emily Bennington, *Author, Coach, Speaker, Leadership Consultant*

2. Breathe and let go. Meditation requires enhanced awareness of breath. Without breath, we cannot sustain life.

"One of the ways we grow is by taking in life and then releasing, letting go the parts that don't work for us. Much like breathing, by holding on and holding in, we become lethargic and unaware. Life then, ultimately, passes us by."

— Molly Rudberg-Leshnock

3. Practice. It's easier than ever to commit to a meditation practice both in your home and at work. No tools, books, or other people are needed for success in this area—just you and ten to thirty minutes of your day. Commit, relax, breathe, and begin. A regular meditation practice will reap huge rewards, including alleviation of anxiety and stress. Many people with a consistent meditation practice report heightened feelings of awareness, happiness, and calm. Not every person feels bliss immediately, but we encourage you to commit to at least one meditation session per week and continue to build from there. Pushing through a session when you don't feel inspired (as you would in strength training) will only increase your "meditation muscle."

Hang in there. You owe it to your mind, body, and spirit.

4. Go on a retreat. Consider attending a meditation retreat or set one up with your colleagues or your peers. This can be a very rewarding experience—one that can open your mind to new ideas and new ways of thinking.

5. Set an intention. Use thoughtful reflection upon one single goal and focus on achieving that goal through your meditation. Bill Ford, Executive Chairman of the Ford Motor Company, says that, during difficult times at his company, he has set an intention to go through each day with compassion.

6. Start slowly ... then build. Ideally, you want to spend at least twenty minutes per day in stillness and meditation, but don't expect to be able to achieve this right away. Meditation and reflection are not easy, so start with just one minute per day of silent reflection. Then work up to three minutes, then five, then ten. Before you know it, you'll be looking forward to each day's session, and you will be more refreshed and more productive as a result.

7. Cultivate an attitude of gratitude. Taking the time to reflect upon what you are grateful for is a wonderful way to meditate and start your day. Besides the obvious mental benefits, being grateful improves your mood and reduces cortisol. Research conducted at the University of California found that people who worked to "cultivate an attitude of gratitude" each day experienced improved mood, increased energy, and overall better physical well-being.

Daily Practice

Here are a few suggestions on how to incorporate these ideas into your daily practice:

— Watch the movie *Miracle*. Notice themes and how they can be incorporated into your life.

— Wake each day and commit to an intention of being at peace.

— Create a meditation habit. Go online and find a free twenty-one-day meditation.

— Write and send (or give away) five notes of gratitude per week.

— Read *Journey of Awakening: A Meditator's Guidebook* by Ram Dass.

— Go to www.tut.com. Take the Adventurer's Challenge and get "Notes from the Universe" daily.

"At the end of the day, I can end up just totally wacky,
because I've made mountains out of molehills.
With meditation, I can keep them as molehills."
—Ringo Starr

A FINAL WORD

We all want more prosperity, happiness, flexibility, and joy in our daily lives. Every day, we are met with challenges, business opportunities, relationships, and tough decisions. They all require clear, confident decision making. How can you expect to go about making these clear decisions when you haven't taken the time to center your mind, body, and spirit? When someone makes rash decisions based on hunches, he or she may get upset when things don't turn out exactly as planned. Some people meet challenges with anger and frustration. Some connect with others while not meeting them in the moment, constantly wondering, "What's coming next? What's in it for me?"

This way of approaching and doing business is over. We are entering a new paradigm where focus, out-of-the box thinking, and strength all take on a new meaning. It's a meaning that is centered and soul-filled. We have learned through our survey, interviews, and personal experiences that the business conversation and landscape requires us to think, feel, and act differently. We must give each other the space to evolve and grow in the workplace—and we can begin this by integrating core yoga principles into our daily business activities.

"Yoga, an ancient but perfect science, deals with the evolution of humanity. This evolution includes all aspects of one's being, from bodily health to self-realization. Yoga means union—the union of body with consciousness and consciousness with

the soul. Yoga cultivates the ways of maintaining a balanced attitude in day to day life and endows skill in the performance of one's actions."

— B.K.S. Iyengar, *Yogi*

Yoga (like life) is a practice, and we are all students. This practice is simple to incorporate into your daily attitude and routine. You don't have to employ all of these techniques at once or even right away. See what works for you and continue to evolve your own personal practice.

We also believe that, by integrating these principles into the daily corporate conversation, we can build smarter, healthier, more efficient organizations—work environments with motivated, healthy individuals who understand their individual impact and place in the whole. We envision individuals who are committed to the corporate world because it is a symbol of health, vitality, and balance. By bringing the yoga mat to the corner office, we can create a more joyful, healthy business environment filled with centered, soulful success.

Namaste—"I bow to the divine in you."

Colophon

Publisher / Editorial Director: Michael Roney

Art Director: Sarah M. Clarehart

Copyeditor: Michelle Ovalle

Proofreader: Joanne Shwed

Contact: info@highpointpubs.com

CPSIA information can be obtained at www.ICGtesting.com
Printed in the USA
LVOW05s0825200315

431332LV00036B/782/P